RUSSIA

Julie Murray

Big Buddy BOOKS
Explore the Countries

VISIT US AT
www.abdopublishing.com

Published by ABDO Publishing Company, PO Box 398166, Minneapolis, MN 55439.

Copyright © 2014 by Abdo Consulting Group, Inc. International copyrights reserved in all countries. No part of this book may be reproduced in any form without written permission from the publisher. Big Buddy Books™ is a trademark and logo of ABDO Publishing Company.

Printed in the United States of America, North Mankato, Minnesota.
032013
112013

PRINTED ON RECYCLED PAPER

Coordinating Series Editor: Rochelle Baltzer
Editor: Sarah Tieck
Contributing Editors: Megan M. Gunderson, Marcia Zappa
Graphic Design: Adam Craven
Cover Photograph: *Shutterstock*: 2bears.
Interior Photographs/Illustrations: *AP Photo*: AP Photo (pp. 15, 17), Eric Gay, pool (p. 29), Sergei Krasnoukhov (p. 25), RIA-Novosti, Alexei Nikolsky, Presidential Press Service (p. 19), Ivan Sekretarev (p. 35); *Getty Images*: Shaun Botterill (p. 37), Imagno (p. 13), Keystone (p. 33), Vasili Andreevich Tropinin (p. 31); *Glow Images*: Luis Castaneda (p. 27), Wolfgang Kaehler (p. 11), SuperStock (p. 16); *iStockphoto*: ©iStockphoto.com/DmitryND (p. 23), ©iStockphoto.com/Pro-syanov (p. 21); *Shutterstock*: Nadezhda Bolotina (p. 23), cloki (p. 5), Asaf Eliason (p. 35), Helen Filatova (p. 9), Globe Turner (pp. 19, 38), JetKat (p. 11), Art Konovalov (pp. 29, 34), Mikhail Markovskiy (p. 35), Maya Morenko (p. 27), Sergey Petrov (p. 34), Poznyakov (p. 38).

Country population and area figures taken from the CIA World Factbook.

Library of Congress Control Number: 2013932176

Cataloging-in-Publication Data

Murray, Julie.
Russia / Julie Murray.
       p. cm. -- (Explore the countries)
ISBN 978-1-61783-817-0 (lib. bdg.)
1. Russia--Juvenile literature.   I. Title.
947--dc23
                                                                              2013932176

RUSSIA

Contents

AROUND THE WORLD

Our world has many countries. Each country has different land. It also has its own rich history. And, the people have their own languages and ways of life.

Russia is a country in both Europe and Asia. What do you know about Russia? Let's learn more about this place and its story!

 **Did You Know?**

Russian is the official language of Russia. It uses different letters than English. In Russian, the word *Russia* is spelled Россия.

4

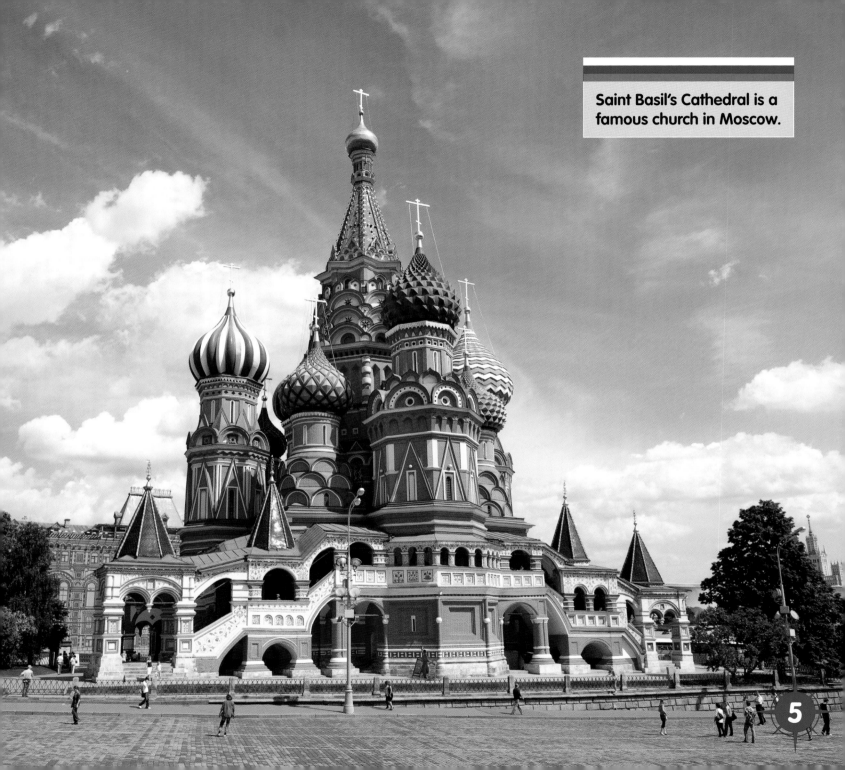

Saint Basil's Cathedral is a famous church in Moscow.

PASSPORT TO RUSSIA

Russia borders 14 other countries. It also borders the Arctic and Pacific Oceans and several seas.

Russia has a total area of 6,601,668 square miles (17,098,242 sq km). That makes it the largest country in the world! More than 142 million people live there.

WHERE IN THE WORLD?

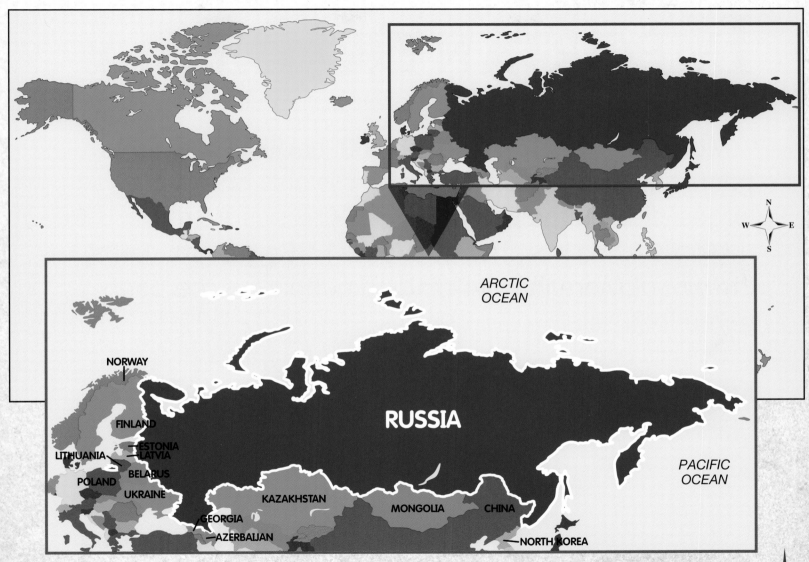

ARCTIC OCEAN

NORWAY

FINLAND

ESTONIA
LATVIA

LITHUANIA

BELARUS

POLAND

UKRAINE

RUSSIA

KAZAKHSTAN

MONGOLIA

CHINA

PACIFIC OCEAN

GEORGIA

AZERBAIJAN

NORTH KOREA

Important Cities

Moscow is Russia's **capital**. With about 11.5 million people, it is Russia's largest city. It is also one of the largest cities in the world.

Moscow first became a city in 1147. By the late 1840s, it was a powerful center of Russia. Moscow has been home to Russia's royal families.

The city is shaped like a wheel. At its center is the Kremlin. This walled area has historic government buildings.

RUSSIA

•Saint Petersburg

★ Moscow

•Novosibirsk

Red Square is just outside the
Kremlin's walls. It has been
home to many military parades.

Did You Know?

Saint Petersburg was Russia's capital from 1712 to 1918.

Saint Petersburg is Russia's second-largest city. It is home to about 4.8 million people. It is in northwest Russia at the mouth of the Neva River.

Novosibirsk is Russia's third-largest city, with about 1.5 million people. It is located on the Ob River in a part of Russia known as Siberia. Many factories there make machines for mining. They also produce trucks.

SAY IT

Novosibirsk
noh-voh-suh-BIHRSK

There are bridges and islands throughout Saint Petersburg.

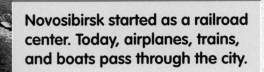

Novosibirsk started as a railroad center. Today, airplanes, trains, and boats pass through the city.

RUSSIA IN HISTORY

The first settlers arrived in what is now Russia thousands of years ago. Around 1240, this area became part of the Mongol Empire. After about 240 years, the Russian people broke away.

In the past, Russia was ruled by **czars**. In 1613, the Romanov family began ruling Russia. There would be 18 rulers from this family.

Over the years, Russian rulers took over much new land. Soon, Russia was large and powerful. In the 1800s, it became known for its authors, music, plays, and ballets.

Peter I began ruling Russia in 1682. He helped the country grow. He became known as Peter the Great.

Did You Know?

Ivan IV became the first czar of Russia in 1547. He was known as Ivan the Terrible because he was cruel.

13

Unhappy with their leadership, Russian people started a **revolution**. In 1918, Nicholas Romanov and his family were killed. He was the last **czar**.

After this, Vladimir Lenin and his followers took power. They formed a **Communist** government. It established the Soviet Union in 1922.

The Soviet Union broke apart in 1991. Russia formed its own government. The people began to rebuild their country.

Did You Know?

Communism allowed Russian people few freedoms. The government had rules about what people could read and do.

Lenin died in 1924. He was honored with a special memorial in Red Square. People can still visit his tomb and see his body today.

Timeline

1869

Leo Tolstoy's *War and Peace* was printed. This became a classic and world-famous book.

1762

Catherine II began ruling Russia. Known as Catherine the Great, she was the country's longest-ruling female leader.

1928

Joseph Stalin began ruling the Soviet Union. He was known as a powerful and cruel leader.

1957

The Soviet Union launched *Sputnik 1* into space. It was the first in the world to do this.

2012

After a heat wave, wildfires burned in eastern Russia. These fires ruined crops and land. They were some of the worst fires on record.

1991

The Cold War ended. This was a time of tension between the United States and the Soviet Union. It had started in 1945.

An Important Symbol

Russia's flag was first used in 1699. Russia had a different flag when it was part of the Soviet Union. When it became independent in 1991, it brought back its own flag.

Today, Russia's government is a **republic**. The president is the head of state. The country's laws are made by the State Duma and the Federation Council.

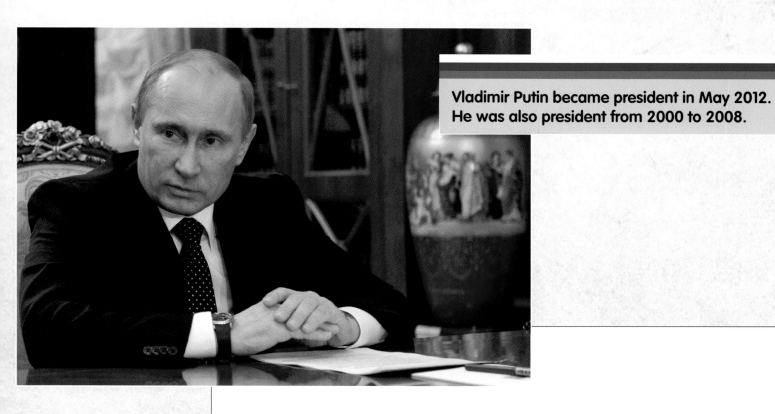

Vladimir Putin became president in May 2012. He was also president from 2000 to 2008.

Russia's flag has three colored bands. The colors have no official meaning.

ACROSS THE LAND

Russia has **tundra**, forests, grassy plains, and mountains. An area called Siberia covers eastern Russia. Rich farmland is found across Russia.

In southern Russia, the Caucasus Mountains are home to Mount Elbrus. At 18,510 feet (5,642 m), this is Europe's highest point. The Ural Mountains divide Europe and Asia.

The Lena and Volga Rivers are known for their length. Russia also has about 200,000 lakes! This includes the world's largest salt lake, the Caspian Sea.

Siberia is known for being very cold. In January, the average temperature in northeastern Siberia is -50°F (-46°C). In July, it is 60°F (16°C).

Many types of animals make their homes in Russia. These include reindeer, arctic foxes, bears, and mouselike jerboas.

Russia is known for its dry, cold land. Parts of Russia are treeless plains. But, trees grow well in other parts of the country. Some of them include fir trees, pine trees, and birch trees.

Both male and female reindeer grow antlers.

Arctic foxes are also called white or snow foxes. They live farther north than any other foxes.

Earning a Living

In the Soviet Union, the government ran factories and farms. This changed when the Soviet Union broke apart.

Today, private businesses operate in Russia. Many people work for the government, hospitals, and schools.

Russia has many natural **resources**. Iron ore and nickel come from its mines. Farmers produce barley, oats, potatoes, rye, and sugar beets. Cattle, hogs, sheep, and goats are raised there.

Did You Know?

Russia is one of the world's largest producers of oil and natural gas.

Fishing is an important business in Russia. Caviar, or fish eggs, is a food that comes from fish living in Russia's seas.

LIFE IN RUSSIA

Russia's people are known for their work in the arts. The country's ballet dancers are famous all over the world! Many of Russia's writers have set stories in Saint Petersburg.

Russia can be a cold, hard place to live. So, Russians are known for eating hearty foods. Most people eat their biggest meal for lunch.

Did You Know?

In Russia, children attend school from about ages 6 to 17.

Borscht is a soup made from beets.

The Nutcracker is a famous Russian ballet.

Russians are known for being powerful athletes. Football, or soccer, is the country's most popular sport. Other favorite sports include basketball, gymnastics, skiing, and tennis.

Russian Orthodox is one of Russia's main religions. Its members believe in Jesus and worship using the Bible. Saints, candles, and religious art are part of their worship.

Russian Orthodox churches are often large and beautifully decorated.

Russian athletes do very well at the Olympic Games. Russia has strong gymnasts and basketball players.

FAMOUS FACES

Many famous people are from Russia. Poet Aleksandr Pushkin was born in Moscow in 1799. His great-grandfather was part of Peter the Great's court.

Pushkin is known as Russia's greatest poet. Some consider him the greatest Russian writer. *Eugene Onegin* is his most famous book. He also wrote many well-known poems. He died in 1837.

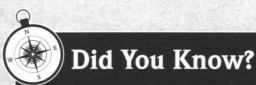

Did You Know?

Pushkin got into many fights called duels. He died when he lost one of them. Many people were sad to lose such a great writer so young.

Pushkin wrote about his love for his wife. He also wrote about the Russian government. Sometimes, his writing got him in trouble.

Sergey Rachmaninoff was born in Oneg in 1873. Around age 12, he began studying piano and music at the Moscow **Conservatory**. In 1892, he won an important award from this school for an opera he wrote.

Rachmaninoff grew up to become a famous **composer**. He is considered one of the world's best pianists. One of his most famous songs is *Prelude in C-Sharp Minor* for piano. He died in 1943.

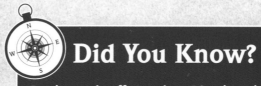

Did You Know?

Rachmaninoff was just 19 when he wrote *Prelude in C-Sharp Minor* for piano.

Rachmaninoff got many ideas from church singers and bells.

Tour Book

Have you ever been to Russia? If you visit the country, here are some places to go and things to do!

 ## See

Watch tigers do tricks at the Moscow Circus! This circus is famous around the world.

 ## Discover

See the Winter Palace in Saint Petersburg. It was home to many Russian royal families. It was finished in 1762.

 # Cheer

Soccer is Russia's most popular sport. Watch a game at the Luzhniki Stadium in Moscow. This stadium was used for the 1980 Olympics.

 # Explore

Visit Lake Baikal in southern Russia. It is the world's deepest lake, at 5,315 feet (1,620 m) deep!

 # Ride

See the country on the Trans-Siberian Railroad. It is the longest railroad in the world! It was started in the 1890s to connect cities in the east and west.

A Great Country

The story of Russia is important to our world. The people and places that make up this country offer something special. They help make the world a more beautiful, interesting place.